Perfect Petals

Photos and Illustrations

By Rebecca Ann Ivy

House of Ivy

ISBN-13: 978-1533541000

ISBN-10: 1533541000

Take a walk with me,

To my favorite place,

A place to find comfort,

A place to find calm,

A place to feel better,

A simple walk in the Park..

and lovely Flowers...

A very refreshing place.

Page 2

Page 3

White Carnation Flowers

Page 4

Page 5

Vine of Ivy

White Clematis Vine

Page 7

White Dandelion

Page 8

Page 9

White and Yellow Daffodil

Page 10

Carolina Jasmine

Page 11

Perfect Pink Roses

Page 13

Doreen Peony

Soft Purple Star Flower

Page 16

Page 17

Periwinkle Myrtle

Page 18

Purple-Bearded Iris

Page 19

Page 20

Pink Lacy Iris

Plush Green Moss

Perfect Pink Azaleas

Page 24

Page 25

Peach Parfait Roses

Page 26

Page 27

Wild Wisteria Vine

Page 28

Ruby Red Roses

Page 29

Page 30

Bright Red Tulip

Page 32

Endless Fields of Indian Paintbrush

Page 33

Page 34

Indian Paintbrush

Page 35

Spider Web after a Fresh Rain

Page 36

Bluebonnet Wildflowers

Page 37

Fragrant Honeysuckle Vine

Page 38

Page 39

Page 40

Orange Sherbert Daylily

Page 41

Field of Soft Clover

Page 43

Page 44

Pink, Purple and Blue Hydrangea

Page 45

Page 46

Page 47

Page 48

Page 49

Pink Impatiens

Page 50

Page 51

Page 52

Lucky Lady Bug

The Heart of the Woods

Page 54

House of Ivy

ISBN-13: 978-1533541000

ISBN-10: 1533541000